"Some years we approach our Lenten disciplines with a sense of enthusiasm; we're ready for the challenge of the desert; we know we will emerge stronger for our time spent thirsting, climbing, and stepping forward in faith. In other years, we may look at Lent with wary eyes, all too familiar with the weight of our faults, and daunted by the bright empty heat into which we must carry them, until we find Jesus, to whom they may be surrendered. Whether you are anticipating Lent as an adventure to be embraced or as a scorching sojourn made in heat and light, *Not by Bread Alone* is the perfectly balanced Lenten companion for your daily contemplation. Mary DeTurris Poust has a peculiar gift for finding the common experiences with which we can all identify and rendering them into profound meditations that are both consoling and instructive—the perfect assist through a season of wandering and hope."

—Elizabeth Scalia, author of *Strange Gods: Unmasking the Idols in Everyday Life and Little Sins Mean a Lot*

"If you have ever fallen short of your Lenten resolutions, take this book with you wherever you go this Lent! Whether waiting at a doctor's office, silently sitting outdoors during your lunch break, or deliberately spending time with Jesus at Adoration, Mary DeTurris Poust's insightful words in *Not by Bread Alone* will walk you through each day's Scripture readings, helping you reflect and meditate on the graces waiting for you during this beautiful season of Lent. Day by day, moment-by-moment, this Lent can, and will, be different."

—María Ruiz Scaperlanda is an award-winning author, including, *The Shepherd Who Didn't Run: Fr. Stanley Rother, Martyr from Oklahoma* and *Rosemary Nyirumbe: Sewing Hope in Uganda*

W9-ASW-427

Not by Bread Alone

Daily Reflections for Lent 2019

Mary DeTurris Poust

LITURGICAL PRESS

Collegeville, Minnesota

www.litpress.org

Nihil Obstat: Reverend Robert Harren, J.C.L., *Censor deputatis.*

Imprimatur: ✠ Most Reverend Donald J. Kettler, J.C.L., Bishop of Saint Cloud, September 5, 2018.

Cover design by Monica Bokinskie. Cover art courtesy of Getty Images.

ISSN: 1552-8782

ISBN: 978-0-8146-4511-6   978-0-8146-4536-9 (ebook)

Introduction

At Mass one morning, a little boy sitting in the second pew with his grandmother pointed to the Stations of the Cross hanging nearby, specifically the ninth station, Jesus falls a third time. A look of confusion and concern came across his face and he furrowed his brow, as he tried to decipher what was going on in that scene. Finally, he said, "He's crying. He's crying." Although most of us were focused on how adorable this little boy was, I found myself looking back over my shoulder at the station to see what he saw: Jesus on the ground, the weight of the cross on his shoulder, a Roman soldier towering over him. This is the journey we are about to begin as we stand on the threshold of Lent today.

The road to Calvary over these forty days will be marked by confusion and concern, sadness, and, yes, even moments of joy —not the passing happiness we think of when we hear the word but pure joy, the kind that resides in our hearts when we put our trust in Jesus. The stories that mark our path from here until Easter are powerful and familiar, sometimes so familiar they fail to move us, or, more accurately, we fail to be moved. We've heard it all before. There's nothing new here. Ah, but God makes all things new, and the Scriptures are alive with the Spirit, who blows through the ancient texts to make a word, a phrase, a scene jump out at the exact moment we need it, if only we'd settle down and pay attention.

We need reminders, someone or something to point out what we're missing. Lent is that reminder, affording us the time and space to go deeper, to sit with stories and let them speak to us as if for the first time. What is calling you to transformation? What speaks to your heart?

On that recent morning in church, in the pew in front of the precocious little boy, was an old man, hunched with age and held up on one side by a younger man, his son, perhaps. The older man was dressed in a beautiful suit, his Sunday best. He stood for every prayer, even though he struggled to make even the slightest move, and his son patiently helped him up and down. It was a beautiful moment, this juxtaposition of young and old, boundless curiosity and fading youth, but with faith and grace swirling around both, around all. Taking in the whole scene that morning, I was moved by the reality of so many people from so many places with so many stories, all hungry for one thing: an encounter with the Divine. The same could be said of our Lenten journey.

We walk this journey together, even if we think we are walking alone. Faith and grace bind us to each other and to our God, and that is the stuff of which pure joy is made. Begin down the path today, and, if you get sidetracked, dust yourself off and begin again, knowing that you have companions, seen and unseen, lifting you up, a communion of saints, in which we all get to stake our claim. Stop, look, listen. Joy is hiding in plain sight, even on the road to Calvary, even on the cross, because joy is not fleeting, joy is not a feeling; joy is the knowledge that we have been saved by Jesus Christ, who invites us to join him on the Way today. Let us begin . . .

Reflections

A Spiritual Tattoo

Readings: Joel 2:12-18; 2 Cor 5:20–6:2; Matt 6:1-6, 16-18

Scripture:
Rend your hearts, not your garments . . . (Joel 2:13)

Reflection: What is it about Ash Wednesday that resonates so deeply with people that even those who have been away from church feel compelled to return and be reminded of their own mortality in the form of an ashen cross? It's more than just ritual or obligation, I think. It's primal—a spiritual practice that brings us back to our very core, that pulls us away from the worldly concerns that typically occupy our time and forces us to face the truth we so often want to avoid: We are dust, and to dust we shall return.

Today, marked with a somber sign of our faith, we go out into the world and bear witness to our broken humanity for all to see. The cross on our forehead is meant to leave a lasting imprint deep within, like a spiritual tattoo that will linger long after we complete this forty-day course correction known as Lent. For us to have any hope of coming out the other side renewed and reborn, change cannot be only skin deep. "Rend your hearts, not your garments," we are reminded in the first reading. The sacrifices and prayers of the season help us clear a path, but we can't stop there, not if we want to experience real transformation. God wants nothing less than our hearts broken open so that he might find a resting place within and make us whole. Yes, the exterior practices are important, but what matters most is what happens unseen within our hearts and souls.

Meditation: What spiritual plans have you made for Lent? Are they more focused on outward sacrifices or inward change? While the former is challenging, the latter can be downright intimidating. And yet, that is what we are called to do. What one thing can you do over the course of the next few weeks that might create a permanent change in your life? What would make you whole? Use the sacrifices and prayers of this season to open your heart, mind, and soul to what God has in store for you.

Prayer: Heavenly Father, guide us in right ways as we begin our Lenten journey. Give us the courage to allow ourselves to be transformed by your love. Help us to use our Lenten sacrifices to dig deep into our spiritual center and carve out a space for you alone.

Where Our Crosses Lead

Readings: Deut 30:15-20; Luke 9:22-25

Scripture:
If anyone wishes to come after me, he must deny himself
and take up his cross daily and follow me. (Luke 9:23)

Reflection: If you've ever been on the receiving end of a
really good sales pitch, you know how hard it can be to say
no. A good salesperson can make you feel like you're just
plain crazy for passing up the deal they have to offer. That
is what makes today's gospel so fascinating. If ever you
thought the people of Jesus' time followed him because they
expected some fabulous perks, this passage would dispel
that notion pretty quickly. Deny ourselves? Daily crosses?
With a sales pitch like that, it's a wonder Jesus had any disciples at all. But there they were, and here we are, following
Jesus, despite the dire warnings and our all-too-human pref-
erence for avoiding suffering at all costs.

We probably don't have to look too deeply into our own
lives to see the crosses we'd rather not have to bear. The illness that can't be cured, the job that's cut, the marriage that
falls apart, the child lost to addiction, any and all of it can
find its way into our lives when we least expect it. Even the
seemingly minor crosses can wear us down over time and
make us wonder if God has forgotten about us along the way.

But wrapped up in Jesus' pitch is an offer we really can't refuse: eternal life. The folks gathered around Jesus couldn't know what was coming after Good Friday, but we do. With 20/20 hindsight, we can see where our crosses lead.

Meditation: Is there a cross in your life that is wearing you out or leaving you feeling alone? Can you turn it over to God? What first step can you take? Maybe it's as simple as telling yourself that for the next fifteen minutes you will not try to control the outcome of anything. Just sit and be present. Maybe it's the difficult challenge of asking someone for help, or for forgiveness. The crosses will inevitably come; we can choose what we do with them.

Prayer: Jesus, Son of God, you knew what it meant to suffer just as we do, in ways we can't imagine. Give us the strength to carry the crosses that cast shadows across our lives and to find meaning in the suffering and graces that flow from the knowledge that we are not alone in our struggles, that you are with us always, until the end of time.

More than Window Dressing

Readings: Isa 58:1-9a; Matt 9:14-15

Scripture:
Would that today you might fast
    so as to make your voice heard on high! (Isa 58:4b)

Reflection: Today's message from Isaiah can be a little disheartening. Only three days into our Lenten fasts and practices, and the prophet makes it pretty clear that our sacrifices alone are not enough. They have to mean something in order to strengthen our connection to God; they cannot exist in isolation, or, even worse, in tension with the rest of our lives.

One of the classic church jokes focuses on the all-too-real rush to beat the next guy out of the parking lot after Mass. "Love your neighbor" goes only so far when we're talking about a quick exit. It's not so different with fasting, at least not according to Isaiah. If we are fighting with others amid our fast, forgetting that the deeper meaning is unity and not simply hunger for hunger's sake, then all is for naught. If the fasting and sacrifice don't change us on a deeper level—make us more compassionate, more generous, more patient, more kind—then we've missed something big along the way. And that's a tough message to hear because in our world of more, more, more, it seems like willingly choosing less should be enough to warrant some sort of reward or affirmation.

But our faith is never about window dressing. God challenges us to go beyond what we think we're capable of. Even if we can't go out onto the streets and literally feed the hungry, can we allow our fasting to open us up to those in need among us right now, those who are hungry maybe not for food but for connection, conversation, love? Feed them.

Meditation: Who are the people in your life who need to be fed? Perhaps it's an older parent who would love a phone call, a spouse who might benefit from a hug, a son or daughter who pretends to be self-sufficient but is still a scared child on the inside, a friend who is starving for companionship. Hunger comes in all forms. Can we use the physical hunger caused by fasting to open up a space inside for those who are hungry for more than food?

Prayer: Gracious God, we stand before you today humbled by our inability to get outside of our own heads and recognize the needs of others. Grant us the wisdom and vision to reach out from our place of comfort into the discomfort that plagues the lives of others.

Radical Faithfulness

Readings: Isa 58:9b-14; Luke 5:27-32

Scripture:
He said to him, "Follow me."
And leaving everything behind, he got up and followed
   him. (Luke 5:27b-28)

Reflection: I always try to imagine myself in the place of the apostles when Jesus first calls them. What made them so willing to "leave everything behind" and follow him, even though it would be quite some time before they fully understood who Jesus was? Would I have been willing to do the same if Jesus posed that question to me? Turns out he is posing that question to me and to you. Unlike Matthew, we don't necessarily have to leave our families and belongings behind, but, if we want to do it right, we do have to be radical about it because, quite frankly, everything about Jesus is radical. We've heard the teachings so often that we might not think so, but when you get down to it, ours is a radical faith and we are called to radical faithfulness. Are we still willing to follow?

What is our modern-day equivalent of Matthew's dilemma? We probably can't walk away from our jobs, but what do we need to walk away from in order to follow Jesus? Maybe we work too much, gossip too much, spend too much, drink too much, and love too little. Maybe we follow in word only and have not yet let the gospel take hold deep within. I often say that if I could really grasp with my human mind the reality of who Jesus is and what he has given to me, my life would change in radical and transformative ways. Yet, here I sit, worrying about office politics and work deadlines and household chores. How can we follow Jesus while remaining present in our everyday lives? That is our challenge.

Meditation: Living the gospel in a radical way will look different for each one of us. For some it may truly mean leaving everything behind to become a priest or religious, or a lay missionary. For others it might mean learning to live radical spirituality and solidarity in the midst of family and coworkers and community. What do you need to leave behind in your life today in order to follow Jesus more fully?

Prayer: Jesus, Son of Justice, you call us to put the ways of this world behind us and follow you with our whole hearts. Give us the courage to recognize what that means for us and to leave behind whatever is holding us back to walk the way you have set out for us.

In Word and Deed

Readings: Deut 26:4-10; Rom 10:8-13; Luke 4:1-13

Scripture:
For one believes with the heart and so is justified,
and one confesses with the mouth and so is saved. (Rom 10:10)

Reflection: The head and the heart don't always like to agree on things. In theory they do, but reality can be a lot more challenging, whether in transcendent spiritual matters or the mundane moments of day-to-day life. I can get up every morning and know in my head that I should spend time in prayer, limit my coffee intake, and eat a healthy breakfast. Otherwise, my spiritual and mental state will be as frazzled as my caffeine- and sugar-addled system. And yet, day after day, I repeat the same less-than-healthy routine: snooze button, multiple cups of coffee, sweets grabbed from the office kitchen. My head knows the healthy routine that could turn those habits around, but the rest of me prefers the comforts that soothe my heart, and so I walk the path worn into the carpet of my soul rather than do what I know is better for me.

Spiritual life is no different. We're reminded today that we have to believe in our heart that Jesus is Lord and confess it with our mouth. It's not an either-or proposition. But what I confess with my mouth doesn't always mirror what's going on in my heart. And vice versa. Sometimes my heart can be moved with compassion but my mouth stays shut, rendering my heart mute as well. If I profess Jesus is Lord but hold onto grudges, my words ring hollow. How do we bring the two together?

Meditation: Only in prayer will we find the common thread that can join heart and head. No words or promises will hold any weight in our being unless and until they are grounded in prayer. God first. God alone. Once we make that our path, all the others will fade away and we will be in sync with ourselves and with our God. Today see if you can bring the hopes in your heart and the words in your head to God and ask for the strength to live what you say and say what you know in your heart to be good and true.

Prayer: Loving Father, our love for you courses through our heart and soul, and yet often our outward lives don't reflect that love or our beliefs. Give us the courage to confess with our mouths the unconditional love and mercy you offer each one of us.

Uncomfortable Compassion

Readings: Lev 19:11-18; Matt 25:31-46

Scripture:
What you did not do for one of these least ones,
you did not do for me. (Matt 25:45b)

Reflection: Even after a lifetime of hearing this verse from Matthew again and again, it still makes me cringe. I have a hard time imagining I won't be shunted off with the goats when it comes time to divide the herd. Not because I don't want to help those in need—I'll throw money in the basket or collect clothes and canned goods whenever asked—but my care and concern for "these least ones" never causes me discomfort. From my warm home with its table laden with too much food and closets bursting with too much stuff, a material donation now and then doesn't seem to rise to the level of what Jesus is asking of his followers.

This past summer, my older daughter, Olivia, left the comfort of her air-conditioned, suburban life to spend a week in Appalachia renovating homes. She returned from West Virginia a changed young woman, set on doing something with her life that would have a direct impact on those suffering in ways she had not previously seen or imagined. Living out this gospel verse for just one week transformed her worldview and her life. Maybe that's the part we forget when we restrict ourselves to comfortable compassion. Serving others is not meant to change only them; it is also meant to change us.

Meditation: We tend to recognize that children benefit from serving others. In fact, it's typically a requirement for confirmation students. We understand that direct service will make them better Christians, better citizens. We seem to forget that we grown-ups could benefit from that same approach. Serving others not only provides for those in need but also transforms our perspective on our own life and on our world. We become more grateful, more compassionate, more generous, more loving when we push out of our comfort zones and into the lives of those on the margins. Can you find a person or project that needs your help this Lent and serve in a way that may cause you a little discomfort even as it opens your heart in new and life-changing ways?

Prayer: Jesus, the Good Shepherd, give us the courage to go to the edges to reach those in need, even if it challenges us, even if it makes us uncomfortable, so that we may truly love our neighbors as ourselves.

March 12: Tuesday of the First Week of Lent

A Matter of Trust

Readings: Isa 55:10-11; Matt 6:7-15

Scripture:
Your Father knows what you need before you ask him.
  (Matt 6:8b)

Reflection: Today's lesson on prayer can seem contradictory. Jesus tells us not to imagine we'll get anywhere in prayer with a lot of words, that God knows what we need before we ask. And then Jesus proceeds to teach us to pray with specific words and to ask for things. So, which is it? Words or no words? Do we bring our needs to the Father or just wait for God to give us what we need? It's both/and, I think. We are human, and so it's only natural that we go to God with words and pleas, but, at the same time, we are called to listen, to wait, to trust. It's not easy. Speaking for myself, I try a little too hard to control things, even in prayer, presenting God with a laundry list of items that need tending.

St. John of the Cross said, "If a man wishes to be sure of the road he treads on, he must close his eyes and walk in the dark." Again, we sense the contradiction that is our prayer life. Pray without speaking, receive without asking, walk without seeing. The words Jesus taught us echo that theme. We pray "thy will be done," which is like walking with our eyes closed. We ask for "our daily bread," not bread for a lifetime, not even bread for the week, just enough for today. The one constant here is trust. Do we trust what God has in store for us, even without asking?

Meditation: What does your usual prayer life look like when you break it down? What is your word-to-silence ratio? Can you increase the latter and listen for God in the silence, trusting that, even without speaking a word, God knows your heart? Today, take the words that Jesus taught us, the Our Father, and speak them aloud at the start of your daily prayer session. Focus on each line with intensity. When you are finished, sit in silence for at least five solid minutes to let those words resonate and to listen for the rustle of the Spirit within your soul.

Prayer: Spirit of Love, speak to me in the silence of my days and breathe God's grace into those places in my life where I hold on too tight, where I refuse to trust. Give me the patience and wisdom to let God be God.

March 13: Wednesday of the First Week of Lent

The Only Sign that Matters

Readings: Jonah 3:1-10; Luke 11:29-32

Scripture:
Just as Jonah became a sign to the Ninevites,
so will the Son of Man be to this generation. (Luke 11:30)

Reflection: We are a people who like signs—literal and figurative. How would we get anywhere these days without the trusty GPS barking out commands as we drive into the unknown? We like things spelled out for us, preferably in flashing neon, and we expect God to do the same. And yet, how often do we ignore the glaring spiritual signposts that dot the landscape of our lives, attempting to lead us on right paths or warn us away from dangerous curves? We ask God to send us a sign, but when we get one, we balk and look for the more convenient sign, the easier way. We think we know better—until we realize we don't.

Like the people of Nineveh, we're not going to come around until someone lands on our doorstep and tells us flat out, and even then we might take issue. But God never gives up on us. Not in Nineveh, not in Galilee, not in our hometown today. God dogs us, relentless in his love, convinced of our goodness, sure that we are worth saving—so sure, in fact, that his Son will die on a cross as a sign of that love. Is there any greater sign than the cross? We hang the cross in our home, wear it around our neck, and still we lose our way. There is only one sign worth heeding. The way of the cross is our way to eternal life.

Meditation: Find a crucifix. Make that the focus of your prayer today. Look at it, meditate on it, hold it in your hand so that its reality is unavoidable. While it's important to have the cross visible in the place where we live and, if possible, at work, the danger is that it becomes part of the background noise, like wallpaper. Today we're going to retrieve the cross from its visual outpost and bring it back to the center of our lives. Keep an eye out for the crosses that are hidden in unlikely places throughout your day. There are signs everywhere, if we're willing to look.

Prayer: Wounded Savior, we thank you for offering your body, your being, your life on our behalf. Forgive us for the times we've taken the cross for granted. Help us, beginning anew today, to live by the sign of the cross, the only way to salvation.

March 14: Thursday of the First Week of Lent

Trust Fit for a Queen

Readings: Esth C:12, 14-16, 23-25; Matt 7:7-12

Scripture:
Save us from the hand of our enemies;
    turn our mourning into gladness
    and our sorrows into wholeness. (Esth C:25)

Reflection: Although our circumstances surely can't match those of Queen Esther in today's first reading, her lament and her prayer certainly sound familiar. Isn't it amazing how these ancient words can ring true for us even though we are separated by centuries and oceans and death itself? Some things are universal, and although some of us will have easier paths than others, wherever we are on this road through life, we will inevitably be tormented by suffering we cannot bear at some point. Oftentimes we'll try to fight through that suffering alone, but Esther reminds us that we do not have to do that. Even if we are all alone on this earth, we are never truly alone. God is always with us.

"Turn our mourning into gladness and our sorrows into wholeness," she prays, as though speaking the words etched on our own hearts. None of us can escape mourning and sorrow, but each of us has a choice about what to do with it and how to face it. Can we turn it over to God and prostrate ourselves before him in complete and utter surrender? Can we, like Esther, ask for the outrageous, the unthinkable, and then wait in trust for the answer to be given? In the gospel, Jesus, too, reminds us that all we need to do is ask, seek, knock, and our heavenly Father will give us every good thing we need.

Meditation: Imagine for a moment that you have the fierce faith of Queen Esther, a prayer warrior if ever there was one. Maybe you already have that kind of unshakable faith. Maybe, like so many of us, you are a little shaky at times when it comes to handing things over to God without reservation. Whatever the case may be, today try to enter the scene in the first reading. Let yourself become part of the story. See yourself with absolute faith in the power of an all-loving God. Now imagine you can take that scene and overlay it on some aspect of your life that requires an extra dose of trust. Let it all go, and rest in God's embrace.

Prayer: God of abundance, we turn to you today in total surrender. Take our burdens and our fears, our sorrows and our hopes. We trust in your grace, in your mercy, and in your constant presence, even when we feel alone.

March 15: Friday of the First Week of Lent

The Anger We Carry

Readings: Ezek 18:21-28; Matt 5:20-26

Scripture:
But I say to you, whoever is angry with his brother
will be liable to judgment . . . (Matt 5:22)

Reflection: Our entire world seems short-fused these days. On a good day it might mean an angry tirade directed at you from a "friend" on social media or from a car in the next lane in a traffic jam. On a bad day it could mean violence erupting right before your eyes or unfolding on TV. A shooting at the one extreme, a shouting match at the other, both of them stemming from the same seed: anger tinged with resentment. After reading about the shooting in Las Vegas that claimed fifty-eight lives and injured hundreds more in late 2017, I sat at my kitchen table in upstate New York, tears streaming down my face, and prayed to be a more peaceful person myself, knowing that peace must begin—as the classic song tells us—with me. We may look at tragic violence and imagine that it remains completely separate from us. We wouldn't shoot anyone. We wouldn't cause harm. Meanwhile, many of us hold anger in our hearts, often over minor offenses. We all have some level of anger, whether we express it or repress it. My anger affects my loved ones and friends; your anger affects your loved ones and friends. And although we may not realize it, our collective anger, both spoken and unspoken, seeps out into the world making it a little less peaceful. So, when you think you can't do anything to stop the violence in the world, think again, and start right where you are. Today, put aside your anger, even if it's seemingly justified, and cultivate peace instead. Do your part to stop the madness.

Meditation: In today's gospel, Jesus makes it clear that anger does not hurt only others; it hurts us. We can't be truly free and forgiven unless we are willing to forgive, and forgiving means letting go of the anger we carry like an albatross around our neck. Is there someone who needs your forgiveness today? Is there a hurt you've been holding onto? What would it take to let that go? Can you make amends and begin the healing process—for yourself, for your loved one, for the world?

Prayer: God of mercy, teach me to forgive others as I wish to be forgiven. Help me to loosen the bonds of anger and resentment that separate me from you and from those around me and to plant seeds of peace in our world.

Grit and Grace

Readings: Deut 26:16-19; Matt 5:43-48

Scripture:
Today you are making this agreement with the LORD:
  he is to be your God and you are to walk in his ways
  and observe his statutes, commandments and decrees,
  and to hearken to his voice. (Deut 26:17)

Reflection: For most of us, the day we accepted the Lord's agreement was on the day of our baptism, most likely as an infant. Someone else stood in as a witness—our parents and godparents—to say, "Yes, we agree to walk in God's way, follow his commandments, and obey his voice." Although there are many out there who have accepted that invitation as adults entering the Church, the vast majority of Catholics did not have to wrestle with the decision consciously, and so, perhaps, we don't remember or realize what a big decision it was and what an enormous responsibility we accepted, or was accepted for us.

Of course, every Sunday at Mass we do, in effect, agree to all of these same requirements and invitations again when we make our profession of faith and answer yes to all the same promises that were asked and accepted at our baptism. Do we enter into that profession with eyes wide open or, as is probably often the case, by rote, spiritually unconscious much of the time? Could we today, in complete honesty, accept the Lord's agreement as outlined in Deuteronomy and echoed in the Gospel of Matthew, the agreement that calls for obedience and complete devotion, that calls for loving everyone, even those who hate us? It's a big undertaking, following the way of God, the way of Jesus Christ, and, although it is offered freely to all, it requires daily recommitment and hard spiritual practice.

Meditation: Pray the creed today—Apostles' or Nicene, your pick. Use it as the spark for daylong meditation and reflection, taking it line by line, piece by piece. Perhaps you can even take one key phrase at the start of every hour and use it as *lectio divina*, turning it over in your heart and mind, looking for messages you may have overlooked or forgotten over the years. There is so much beauty in this prayer, the outline of our whole faith written so succinctly, a pocket-size prayer that encompasses all. Yes, Lord, I believe, I agree, I accept; help me follow.

Prayer: Father, Son, and Spirit, I place myself before you today, ready to reaffirm my beliefs and recommit myself to the way you ask me to walk. Give me the resolve to recognize the grit and grace I will encounter when I enter into this agreement with all my heart.

Spiritual Sleepwalking

Readings: Gen 15:5-12, 17-18; Phil 3:17–4:1 or 3:20–4:1;
Luke 9:28b-36

Scripture:
Peter and his companions had been overcome by sleep,
    but becoming fully awake,
    they saw his glory and the two men standing with him.
        (Luke 9:32)

Reflection: I've spent most of my life anticipating the moment when I might become "fully awake" and recognize God undeniably present in my life in some monumental way akin to what Peter, James, and John experience on Mount Tabor. I desperately want my own version of the transfiguration, complete with a voice from the clouds telling me beyond the shadow of a doubt that God is right there with me. I don't think that's in the cards for me, or for most of us, and yet we are called to believe just the same. That's the essence of faith.

That doesn't mean we won't long for a little positive reinforcement along the way now and then, preferably of the concrete variety that can't be mistaken. A miracle, maybe, or at least a coincidence that is clearly more than a random occurrence. We search for roses and butterflies, feathers and dragonflies that we declare to be the sign we are seeking—of a loved one long gone, of God's approval of a decision, of the Spirit buoying us up when we are sinking. In those brief moments we are suddenly awake and aware, and then, just as suddenly, we fall asleep again and forget that God is still present even when the signs are not. Even Peter was not immune. It would not be long after the mountaintop experience that he would deny even knowing Jesus and lock himself away in fear and shame, a wake-up call of the most painful kind.

Meditation: There's nothing wrong with seeking signs and symbols to remind us of God's presence. For some it might be the beauty of a sunrise over the ocean, for another the sound of a newborn baby crying, for others the sight of a rainbow arching overhead. Anything that calls us back to our spiritual core, the divine amid daily life, is a good thing, but often it takes more than that, a crisis or a loss, to wake us up to the faith that sustains us. We want dazzling lights and parting clouds, but sometimes our aha moments come to us through tears, though pain, through failure.

Prayer: God of all creation, you make all things new. You are at once transfigured and transfiguring. Open our eyes to your presence in our lives. Wake us from the spiritual slumber that keeps you hidden from us. Make us new.

A Recipe for Healing

Readings: Dan 9:4b-10; Luke 6:36-38

Scripture:
For the measure with which you measure
   will in return be measured out to you. (Luke 6:38b)

Reflection: I've never been much of a baker. I don't like all the measuring that's required. I prefer recipes where I can swap things out, where I can toss and sprinkle with abandon rather than scoop and level with precision. To me, baking is much more difficult than cooking. Yes, there is a clear set of instructions, but there's no wiggle room. Which is why today's gospel makes me a little uncomfortable. It's measuring taken to a whole new level, one that could have eternal ramifications.

We like to think God will measure out heaping servings of forgiveness and mercy when it comes to our own wrong-doings so long as we're sincerely sorry, but today's gospel warns that unless we are willing to offer the same to others, we could be in for a rude awakening. "Stop judging and you will not be judged." It sounds so simple on the surface, but we're likely to encounter the urge to judge before we even leave our house in the morning, maybe even before we leave our bed. News headlines, social media posts, work e-mails, and more can leave us judging and condemning before we've even had our first sip of coffee. It's become something of a national sport.

So how do we step outside the fray and withhold judgment, even when we feel justified? It's not easy, but it is necessary, for our soul's sake and for our sanity's sake. Holding onto grudges hurts us as much as it hurts others. Let go, and see what freedom feels like.

Meditation: When was the last time you gave yourself a hard time? Maybe you made a stupid mistake, said the wrong thing, hurt someone's feelings, or worse. Chances are you replay that moment over and over, holding onto the guilt and shame. If you won't or can't forgive yourself, it becomes very difficult to forgive others. We can't love others unless we love ourselves. So often real change starts right here, with each one of us. Can you forgive yourself for one thing today? Can you forgive someone else tomorrow? Don't start with the biggest mistake. Start with something small, something doable. Train with small things first.

Prayer: Merciful Lord, fill my heart with compassion and love as I strive to become someone who forgives and embraces rather than someone who clings and condemns. Help me to take the first step toward healing past hurts.

March 19: Saint Joseph, Spouse of the Blessed Virgin Mary

The Space Between

Readings: 2 Sam 7:4-5a, 12-14a, 16; Rom 4:13, 16-18, 22; Matt 1:16, 18-21, 24a or Luke 2:41-51a

Scripture:
When his parents saw him,
   they were astonished,
   and his mother said to him,
   "Son, why have you done this to us?
Your father and I have been looking for you with great
   anxiety." (Luke 2:48)

Reflection: Most parents probably hear this gospel reading and think, "If Mary and Joseph can lose the Son of God for three days, we're doing okay in the child-rearing department." Of course, we've all heard the explanations of this story that make it not only understandable but also likely. Jesus was at an age when his mother may have thought he was walking with the men, but he was still young enough that his father may have thought he was safe with the women. How often has that happened to any one of us? Twenty-one years after the fact, I still have seared into my brain the time we "lost" our son for about thirty seconds in a Toys R Us. Our reaction was probably not unlike that of Mary and Joseph: "Why have you done this to us?"

Today, on the Feast of Saint Joseph, it's a good time to remember the very real challenges Joseph and Mary faced as they raised Jesus. There were probably times when they felt overwhelmed, not up to the monumental task before them, and still they kept the faith. Joseph, in his stoic and strong silence, led them to each next step on the journey God had set before them. Listening, always listening for God's instructions. We remind our children again and again to listen to us, to follow our instructions, but do we, like Joseph, take the time to do the same when the Father speaks to us?

Meditation: In a world where strength and power are often equated with those who speak the loudest or attract the biggest following, Joseph reminds us that quiet strength and unshakable faith are the real power base for a life well-lived. Although he has few scenes in Scripture, his stamp on salvation is undeniable, all because he was willing not only to listen to the voice of God, but also to do what was asked, even when it seemed impossible. Try on quiet strength for size today and see how it changes the dynamic of your own life.

Prayer: Faithful Saint Joseph, we turn to you today, amid the noise and chaos of the world, to ask for your help in becoming more peaceful, more grounded, more open to the voice of God speaking to our hearts. Walk with us as we strive to seek out the space between words and action, the gap where the Spirit speaks.

Win, Place, or Show

Readings: Jer 18:18-20; Matt 20:17-28

Scripture:
[W]hoever wishes to be great among you shall be your servant; whoever wishes to be first among you shall be your slave.
   (Matt 20:26)

Reflection: Ever since we were little kids lining up on the playground, first has equaled best. We want to come in first place; we want our children to take first prize—in the science fair, gymnastics competition, spelling bee, life. Go for the gold, we're told, and we do, with every fiber of our being. That's not necessarily a bad thing—until it becomes the only thing. What if we come in third? What if our child doesn't place at all? What if we come in last, or choose to hand out water at the marathon rather than run?

The message Jesus gives the apostles then and us today is miserable by society's standards. Wanting to be first gets us nowhere when it comes to the spiritual footrace. Serving, stepping back, choosing to be last is our calling, but how do we pull that off when our jobs, our families, our world expect more? It has to do with attachment. It doesn't mean we slack off at our jobs or tell our kids not to try. It means we stop hanging our worth on those "accomplishments" and let go of the need to succeed, at least by worldly standards. When we loosen our grip on the whip that we keep cracking in order to gain more ground, we stop worrying so much about nosing out the next guy and notice the person limping along behind us. When we stop and offer to carry them, we may not cross the finish line first, but we cross it best.

Meditation: What does first place look like in your life? Is it a promotion or a bigger home? A child earning a scholarship or a spouse winning a spot on the city council? What if first place doesn't materialize? Can you be happy with second or third or last? Is there a place in your life where you can opt out of the race and take a new approach, one as servant? When you choose that, notice if serving happens to feel more like winning that first place ever did.

Prayer: Jesus, you show us by example what it means to serve first, always. Give us the courage to see beyond the confines of the culture to the prize you offer us today: achieving salvation not by wit or strength or speed but by gentleness, kindness, and compassion.

Power of Persuasion

Readings: Jer 17:5-10; Luke 16:19-31

Scripture:
Then Abraham said,
   "If they will not listen to Moses and the prophets,
   neither will they be persuaded
   if someone should rise from the dead." (Luke 16:31)

Reflection: I often wonder what it would have been like to hear Jesus preach firsthand, to watch water turned into wine, loaves and fishes multiplied just when we were feeling hunger pangs, the sick healed, the blind with sight restored. Surely it would have stopped me in my tracks. No question about it: I would have left everything behind and followed him. Or would I? Many who saw and heard did not believe, and some even called for his crucifixion. The miracles and the message were not enough to change hearts of stone—which is kind of the point of the end of today's gospel verse. If Moses himself and a string of powerful prophets were not enough to change hearts, why should we think resurrection would make a difference?

Turns out it sometimes doesn't. Every time we gather around the table for Mass, we celebrate death and resurrection: Jesus' two thousand years ago and ours some unknown time in the future. We profess, we believe, and yet we still rage at the first person who crosses us or cuts us off. How quickly resurrection pales next to our human penchant for exacting our fair share. If we take the time to listen, there are prophets among us. They may grab our attention for a day or two, but then the message becomes too difficult to hear and we move on, hoping another prophet will say something we can get behind. But all the true prophets lead us to the same place: Heaven via Calvary. No wonder we try to ignore them.

Meditation: When was the last time you heard a homily or read a story or witnessed an event that made you say, "Jesus is right here in the midst of this"? I bet that for the rest of that day, maybe longer, you kept coming back to those words or that moment, sure it had transformed your life in some permanent way. How soon after did you return to "normal," rushing through life as if tomorrow were guaranteed? What would it take to change you once and for all? Is resurrection enough?

Prayer: God of the prophets, open our ears to those who speak your word in ways that are not always easy to accept. Give us the willingness to put our fears aside and listen with our hearts to the message that might save our souls.

March 22: Friday of the Second Week of Lent

Agents of Love

Readings: Gen 37:3-4, 12-13a, 17b-28a; Matt 21:33-43, 45-46

Scripture:
Therefore, I say to you,
   the Kingdom of God will be taken away from you
   and given to a people that will produce its fruit.
      (Matt 21:43)

Reflection: Looking out for #1. That's the name of the American game. And even if we're not physically harming anyone, a la the tenants in today's gospel parable, we do our share of seizing and stoning in all sorts of figurative ways. Social media alone has become a virtual playground where bullying and verbal stonings occur in comment sections over the most seemingly uncontroversial posts. Email and texting, meetings and committees have their own, perhaps less-public, versions of the same mean-spiritedness. At the core of it is a hardness of heart. We stop seeing things from any perspective but our own.

What would it take to flip that, to soften our hearts and open our minds to the stunning fact that everyone—from our most beloved family member to our most despised enemy—is grappling with some deep-seated insecurities, issues, heartaches, and suffering? It doesn't matter what they look like on the outside; inside there are scars, maybe even open wounds, in need of healing.

St. Teresa of Avila said, "Christ has no body now but yours, no hands, no feet on earth but yours. Yours are the eyes through which he looks with compassion on this world." Unless and until we see ourselves as carrying Christ out into the world, *being* Christ to others, we are likely to keep slipping back into the role of the angry tenants, always seeking to improve our own lives on the back of someone else.

Meditation: Take a few moments for some serious honesty with yourself. When was the last time you looked at someone else and felt a twinge of anger or jealousy over their life, looks, family, achievements? It's not easy to admit, but most of us probably feel that twinge daily. In fact, it's probably so ingrained that we don't even notice it. A photo scrolls by in our Facebook feed and somewhere something registers within us: Why don't I have that? We take a less-than attitude in life, and everyone suffers because of it. Flip that feeling. Today, every time you encounter someone or something that sets off that twinge, bless it. Send light and love to a person who typically causes you sorrow and strife. Be Christ, and be transformed.

Prayer: Generous God, we know your love is abundance made real. Soften our hearts of stone so that we, too, can be agents of love in our daily lives.

March 23: Saturday of the Second Week of Lent

At the Water's Edge

Readings: Mic 7:14-15, 18-20; Luke 15:1-3, 11-32

Scripture:
You will cast into the depths of the sea all our sins. (Mic 7:19)

Reflection: This past summer was the first time in a long time that I did not make it to the New Jersey shore to stand on the wet sand and stare out at the vastness of the ocean. Having grown up on the East Coast, I have been spoiled forever by a proximity to an ocean I have long taken for granted, until this year when I missed my window of ocean opportunity.

Today's first reading from Micah brought those feelings rushing back and reminded me why I love the ocean so much. In that deep sea stretching endlessly toward the horizon, God is palpably present. Throw a stone or shell out into the surf and it disappears, pulled out by the strength of water churning in a constant ebb and flow. If you stand at the water's edge, every wave that crashes to the shore will both wash you clean and anchor you firmly in one place despite the shifting sand around you.

In both readings today, we hear that God's mercy toward us is the same. Our worst sins disappear in the vast ocean of God's mercy. No matter how far we stray, God forgives and forgets, welcoming us back every time, over and over, with the same joy showered on the Prodigal Son, and grounding us in his unshakable love despite the churning chaos of the world around us. How great is our God?

Meditation: Even if you've never been to the ocean, you likely understand the power of it, and maybe you have your own visible reminder of God's great mercy. Perhaps it's the sky, the stars, a vast field of wheat, a great lake or waterfall, or even a busy highway that heads into a gorgeous sunset. What burden are you carrying that needs to be cast off? Give it to God—through the sacrament of reconciliation, through prayer, through penance, and maybe even through some gesture that will remind you in a physical way that God has cast your sin into the depth of the sea that is his Sacred Heart. Toss a rock into the ocean or throw a paper into a fire, and remember that God does likewise with your sins.

Prayer: Merciful and all-loving God, help me to accept your forgiveness and release the burdens that continue to hold me down. Wash me clean; set me free.

March 24: Third Sunday of Lent

Sacred Line in the Sand

Readings: Exod 3:1-8a, 13-15; 1 Cor 10:1-6, 10-12; Luke 13:1-9

Scripture:
Come no nearer!
Remove the sandals from your feet,
   for the place where you stand is holy ground. (Exod 3:5)

Reflection: I'll be the first one to admit that I often approach God without much fear. I whine and complain, demand and plead, like a teenager who's angling for extended curfew hours or the keys to the family car. And while that can often be a good thing—seeing God as a loving parent who will put up with pretty much anything—there can be danger there. We can lose sight of holy ground, of the great I AM, who is and was and is to come.

The burning bush in today's first reading reminds us that God enters into our lives in the ordinariness of our days. Moses was just tending his father-in-law's flock when God burst onto the scene—literally—and called to him. Although none of us get that level of drama in our God moments, they are there, hidden in plain sight, as God waits for us to respond, "Here I am." For us to recognize those entry points, those flashes of the divine in our own daily lives, we have to have an awareness of the holy ground on which we tread, a sense of awe for God's greatness. Sadly, I think we've lost that sense of awe, so cynical are we about so much in our world and so convinced of our own greatness. What sign is calling you to connection?

Meditation: So often, we listen to Scripture stories, such as that of the burning bush in today's first reading, and brush them off as an event meant for a different people in a different time, but the word of God is alive and meant for us today, right now. Look around your life. Is there a figurative burning bush trying to get your attention? Where is your holy ground? During this Lenten season, can you rekindle a sense of awe for the divine and begin to take note of the ordinary moments that provide for extraordinary insights? Where is God in those moments? Or, perhaps more accurately, where are you? There is a saying circulating in spiritual memes and columns that seems to fit here: If God feels far away, guess who moved?

Prayer: Praise to you, God of all creation! May we always be mindful of the holy ground on which we tread, and may we be attentive to your call and open to your invitation.

March 25: The Annunciation of the Lord

The Path of Yes

Readings: Isa 7:10-14; 8:10; Heb 10:4-10; Luke 1:26-38

Scripture:
But she was greatly troubled at what was said
   and pondered what sort of greeting this might be.
Then the angel said to her,
   "Do not be afraid . . . " (Luke 1:29-30)

Reflection: Most of the time, when we reflect on the Annunciation readings and Mary's fiat, her yes to God, we focus on Mary's willingness to put her own fears and concerns aside and follow God's plan, and with good reason. After all, if Mary had done otherwise, salvation history would have hung in the balance. She said yes to God's great challenge and call, and yet she also didn't jump at the chance without hesitation. "She was greatly troubled . . . " We don't know what that looked like in Mary's life or how long that troubled feeling lasted. We get the scriptural CliffsNotes version of Mary's response, but that one brief line opens up a much deeper and, quite frankly, comforting conversation.

   Mary was human, and so, of course, she was "greatly troubled." Why do we so often forget that part and imagine that Mary made this decision with anything more than complete faith in God and the words of an angel? She had no advance details, no assurances, no timeline or guarantees.

That probably sounds familiar, doesn't it? When was the last time you were confronted with a question, a problem, a choice that required faith and trust despite the great unknown that loomed ahead of you? Probably not that long ago. Life often requires us to face things we do not want to face, to go places we do not want to go, to say yes when we'd really rather say no and avoid the challenges.

Meditation: What is causing you to be greatly troubled? Is it a problem at work or with your children? Financial worries or health concerns? Any one of us on any given day has reason to be troubled over something. How we long to be able to say no to those problems, to run in the opposite direction. What would happen if we follow Mary's lead instead and say yes to God and to whatever is causing us to lose sleep? "Be not afraid," the angel tells Mary. We are challenged to do the same, to give our fiat, even in the face of fear.

Prayer: Holy Mary, we look to your example as we strive to answer the questions God has placed before us. Be a model for us and guide us along the path of acceptance and trust, the path that leads to your Son.

March 26: Tuesday of the Third Week of Lent

Pay It Forward

Readings: Dan 3:25, 34-43; Matt 18:21-35

Scripture:
So will my heavenly Father do to you,
  unless each of you forgives your brother from your
    heart. (Matt 18:35)

Reflection: We all owe somebody something, whether it's a literal loan on a car or house or something more ethereal, like the "debts" we owe to those who help us in so many ways—the person who introduces us to someone who eventually gives us a job, the friend who drops off dinner when a family member is ill, the neighbor who shovels our sidewalk during a blizzard. We need each other, probably more than we care to realize or admit, so much so that our eternal salvation hinges upon how we act in relation to each other. That's quite a connection.

Today's gospel parable is somewhat stunning on the surface level. We may read it and think, "How dare that man demand payment of a loan when his own larger debt was forgiven?" If we're honest, we can probably see where we do the same thing in less obvious ways. Every day we are given the chance to let something slide, to forgive, to accept, to encourage, whether it's in a traffic jam or a classroom or a boardroom or our living room. But we humans tend toward self-preservation, which often manifests in grudges, backbiting, and fear-based responses that make us much more like the unforgiving servant than the magnanimous king.

Jesus puts it plainly: You will not receive what you refuse to give. Or, in the language of our times: Pay it forward.

Meditation: Think about the debts you owe. What would it be like if someone said, "All is forgiven; you owe nothing"? Imagine that feeling. Now contemplate the biggest debt you are owed. Would you be able to turn around and forgive it without hesitation? Could you do it even if your own debts were not forgiven first? What might hold you back? Now look at your inner life, the places where you are weighed down by things you feel have not been forgiven by others. What would it feel like to be free of that for good and for ever? Could you offer that to someone who is bound by a debt you have not yet forgiven? Take a chance. Offer forgiveness, and free yourself at the same time.

Prayer: God of compassion, teach us to unclench our fists and open our hands and hearts to those who need our forgiveness and love so that we may, in turn, be open to your merciful embrace.

Spiritual Scrapbook

Readings: Deut 4:1, 5-9; Matt 5:17-19

Scripture:
However, take care and be earnestly on your guard
    not to forget the things which your own eyes have seen,
    nor let them slip from your memory as long as you live
    . . . (Deut 4:9)

Reflection: My children love looking at old photographs from not only their own childhoods, but also mine and my husband's, their grandparents', and even their great-grandparents'. Although technology allows us to capture more images than ever before, there is something special about holding a faded photograph in your hand and stepping back into your history for even the briefest time.

Our memories, for better or worse, shape us, guide us, and sometimes haunt us. But always we remember, for we know that our history gives us clues to what we should or perhaps shouldn't do, to living our lives to the fullest, and to ensuring our family's happiness to the best of our ability. The same holds true for our spiritual memories, truths, and touchpoints. In both readings, from Deuteronomy and the gospel, we are reminded that we cannot forget—specifically, we cannot forget God's laws and expectations because they serve as the guideposts that will lead us to the kingdom of heaven. We must pull these rules out on a regular basis, like old family recipes and rituals, to review them and pass them on to the next generation so that they, too, will know where to look as they make their way along the path of life.

Sometimes we can get lazy or arrogant and bypass the rules. We think we know better—until we don't. Something happens that stops us in our tracks, and suddenly we are digging through our memories in search of the rule, the ritual, the recipe that will get us right with God and right with ourselves.

Meditation: We often bristle at the idea that we have to obey a set of rules. Can't I just be a good person? Why do I need to follow these commandments? If we're willing to reflect on those commandments, however, it becomes clear pretty quickly that the rules lay out a course for our best life. Is there anything unnecessary, wrong, misguided on that list? Nope. Although it may feel like Jesus is scaring us into obeying, he's really doing what he knows is best for us, his willful children who keep trying and failing to figure it out on our own.

Prayer: Jesus our Brother, you know our human weaknesses, our desire to go our own way. Help us to remember your teachings and to follow the only way that leads to happiness.

March 28: Thursday of the Third Week of Lent

Be Still and Know . . .

Readings: Jer 7:23-28; Luke 11:14-23

Scripture:
Listen to my voice;
  then I will be your God and you shall be my people.
    (Jer 7:23)

Reflection: When I went on a much-needed spiritual retreat a few months ago, the Trappist monk who served as my confessor and spiritual director gave me a penance that made me snap to: spend thirty minutes in the presence of God every night for six weeks straight. Notice that he didn't simply say "in prayer," but rather "in the presence of God." He recognized that for someone like me—so easily distracted by too many things on my plate—there is a difference between saying a prayer and being present. In order to spend time "in the presence of God," I had to shut out everything else, even words, and just be. I would begin by reading a Scripture verse or Night Prayer and then just listen for God's voice in all of it. Sure, my mind would wander now and then, and I would try to lead it back to where God was waiting, but, all in all, that half hour of silence each night was an unexpected gift of peace, tranquility, and connection to the divine.

Our world doesn't give us a lot of opportunities for that kind of quiet time with God. It seems luxurious, selfish even, to steal away for a chunk of time and do nothing more than sit and listen for the still small voice of the Spirit. But in this distraction-filled world of ours, that is what we need more than anything else: time apart, a place where nothing comes between us and God.

Meditation: Listen to what's going on around you right now. What do you hear? Now find a place where you can have complete silence. It's still noisy, isn't it? Our minds don't like to settle into the quiet; they shift into overdrive, coming up with all sorts of thoughts and memories and worries to keep us from entering fully into that listening place. God beckons us: "Be still and know that I am God." Can you make regular time to sit quietly and listen for God's voice each day? What if you scheduled your listening time on your calendar? What if you made a date with God?

Prayer: Come to us in the silence, Lord. Let us recognize your voice calling to us amid the noise and chaos of the world around us.

What's Your Question?

Readings: Hos 14:2-10; Mark 12:28-34

Scripture:
And no one dared to ask him any more questions.
   (Mark 12:34**)**

Reflection: Every now and then someone in the crowd has the courage to ask Jesus a question. Sometimes it's an intentionally misleading or confusing question; other times it's a simple and sincere question. But always there's something big about to be revealed. Jesus doesn't make small talk. He makes life-altering pronouncements: Give away everything you have and follow me. Let the dead bury the dead. Or, as in today's gospel, love God above everything else and love your neighbor as yourself, distilling the Hebrew commandments down to one great commandment: love.

   I'm guessing that caused a seismic shift, changing the spiritual playing field with a teaching so basic it was confounding. As if that wasn't enough, Jesus then tells the scribe that his understanding of the teaching makes it clear he is "not far from the Kingdom of God." What does that mean? Apparently, the moment was so significant that no one dared ask. We get the sense they are in awe, possibly a little afraid, certainly unsure of what might happen next. Sounds familiar, doesn't it? So often we let our fear and uncertainty keep us from getting to the heart of what God is calling us to do and be. We get in our own way, afraid to hear God's answer to the questions burning in our hearts. Like the people in the crowd, we don't dare ask a question, lest we find the answer too demanding. Love your neighbor as yourself. Today's gospel teaching is as shocking now as it was then. What does it mean to really live that way? Is it even possible? And if we have not yet figured out how to love ourselves as made in God's image, how can we ever truly love our neighbor?

Meditation: If you could ask Jesus any question, what would it be? Would you have the courage to ask it if you were transported back in time to the scene of today's gospel? We can go to Jesus with our questions in prayer even now. Don't be afraid. Ask the question that weighs on your heart and be confident that, no matter the answer, love will be at its core.

Prayer: Jesus, we come to you today with unspoken questions that long for answers. Calm our fears, hear our prayers, and fill our hearts with gentle love not only for our neighbors, but for ourselves as well.

Code Blue

Readings: Hos 6:1-6; Luke 18:9-14

Scripture:
. . . for everyone who exalts himself will be humbled,
and the one who humbles himself will be exalted.
   (Luke 18:14)

Reflection: If you ever want to feel humbled, check into an emergency room on a busy holiday weekend. From my bed in our local ER, where I spent nine hours one Saturday waiting to be admitted to the cardio unit for chest pains, I could hear nurses and doctors discussing patients in various stages of injury, disease, and dying. One needed a blood transfusion, one had a ruptured ectopic pregnancy, one needed a CT scan for head trauma, another was in heart failure with cancer on top, and another was laid out on a stretcher in a hallway because there were no more open beds. Tethered to machines, our privacy laid bare—literally—as hospital gowns flapped this way and that, none of us were in control. We had to accept that we were going to be poked and prodded, wheeled here and there, told when we could eat and when we could leave—if we could leave.

We don't like to be humbled; it feels like a smackdown or a failure. And yet, when we are forced to enter into that space through circumstances beyond our control, it can open our eyes and our hearts to the struggles of those around us. Suddenly our pride and ego and desire for control are in the spotlight, and we realize that perhaps a little humility might do us some good. Perhaps being "exalted" isn't all it's cracked up to be. The famed Trappist monk Thomas Merton wrote, "Pride makes us artificial, and humility makes us real." Are you willing to be real?

Meditation: It can be hard to let down our guard and be vulnerable, real, humble. It feels scary, like we're opening ourselves up for judgment, pain, and heartache, but it's only when we're willing to go to that vulnerable place that we can uncover our true self, the person God created us to be. What masks do you wear? What would it feel like to remove the mask and reveal the soft, kind, humble you that lies behind it?

Prayer: Heavenly Father, we lay before you our masks, our pride, our weariness at having to clutch and claw for power and prestige, our fear of being vulnerable and exposed. Give us the grace to drop below the surface to the place where the Spirit dwells within and find the gifts that have been buried there for too long.

Clean Slate

Readings: Josh 5:9a, 10-12; 2 Cor 5:17-21; Luke 15:1-3, 11-32

Scripture:
Whoever is in Christ is a new creation:
   the old things have passed away;
   behold, new things have come. (2 Cor 5:17)

Reflection: Every so often I pull out an old journal and read entries from years before. I want to see that I've made "progress" or find some insight I've forgotten about. More often than not, I realize that I'm on a continuous loop. Change the date and it just as easily could have been written today. The last time I did this exercise, I considered tossing the journals, or perhaps having a ceremonial burning, because we cannot grow as human beings or as disciples if we are forever looking back over our shoulder for what was or what might have been.

"Old things have passed away." It's hard to accept that sometimes, a fact that hit me hard when I was picking up a book at the library recently. As I was leaving, a group of moms and toddlers were coming in for story time. At first, the sight made me smile, and then suddenly there were tears in my eyes. I was transported to that time in my own life, wishing I could go back and hold it, savor it, taste it for just a minute. But we do not become new creations by clinging to what was. God calls us into the now. And that can be difficult, especially as we age and the fleetingness of life surrounds even happy moments with the fragrance of melancholy. Jesus does not leave us there, however. He holds out the promise of forgiveness and salvation and makes all things new.

Meditation: We can't let ourselves get so caught up in the past that we live in fear of the here and now. It's tempting. If we have happy memories, the past can feel like a cozy cocoon wrapping us in a vision of yesterday that is rosier than reality. Jesus asks us to step forward in faith, to become new in him. Try to visualize yourself as a new creation. What does that look like? How does it feel? What do you need to do today, this Lent, to become that new creation? The sacrament of reconciliation is a good start. Make plans to get to confession before Lent is over.

Prayer: Merciful Lord, thank you for sending us your Son to free us from sin and make us new. Help us to look forward in hope to the life without fear that you have planned for us.

Make a Note

Readings: Isa 65:17-21; John 4:43-54

Scripture:
Jesus said to him, "Unless you people see signs and wonders, you will not believe." (John 4:48)

Reflection: At one point, when I was working on this book of reflections, I was fighting against my own spiritual darkness even as I prayed and wrote. I had just finished the reflection about the burning bush, the one in which I suggest you look for flashes of the divine in everyday life, when my daughter texted me and asked me to pick her up at school. A few minutes later, as I drove the regular route, the one I've driven too many times to count, I slowed for a red light, and there, nailed to the telephone pole directly to the right of my bumper, was a sign scrawled in simple black marker: "Have faith. Doubt not." I think I actually gasped when I saw it, a message so blatant it verged on ridiculous. When I reached the school parking lot, I took out my smartphone and wrote down what happened in the notes section so I wouldn't forget.

In today's gospel, Jesus seems a little peeved as he talks about the sad fact that even signs and wonders won't make us believe. We are a demanding lot, always needing God to prove his love. Jesus tells the official, "You may go; your son will live": an outrageous sign delivered in a manner so understated that it almost slips by us. Ah, yes, another healing. And then we sit back and wait for something bigger and better to really convince us. Meanwhile, God fills our lives with signs and wonders and waits for us to slow down long enough to spot them. Have faith. Doubt not.

Meditation: The next time some ordinary event or sign takes you aback, makes you gasp, or just slows you down for a minute or two, take note. Literally. Write it down on a piece of paper, this thing or person or situation that presented itself at just the right moment. Or, if you don't have paper, say it out loud. Make it concrete. Etch it on your soul so you can pull it out the next time you're feeling alone and abandoned, the next time you're waiting for a sign.

Prayer: You know our hearts, Jesus. You know we are fickle and forgetful when it comes to your love. Show us the way to true belief, the kind of belief that requires no outer signs because our inner faith is so strong.

A Little Unwell

Readings: Ezek 47:1-9, 12; John 5:1-16

Scripture:
When Jesus saw him lying there
   and knew that he had been ill for a long time, he said
    to him,
"Do you want to be well?" (John 5:6)

Reflection: Imagine if Jesus came upon you in your current situation. Maybe you're at your desk working or at home caring for children. Maybe you're confined to bed due to illness, or running errands, or running just for fun. Regardless of our health, there's a pretty good chance we need healing of some sort. Jesus, who would see right through our façade, would know that some part of us is broken or hurting, and he might ask us, as he does the sick man in today's gospel, "Do you want to be well?" We would likely answer, "Of course!" Or would we, like the sick man, talk about all the reasons we wish we could be well but can't because other people are making it impossible for us?

The wellness Jesus offers has nothing to do with the state of our physical body and everything to do with the health of our soul. Do we want to be well? We say yes even as we put up walls to keep out God's healing grace. We keep at the behaviors we know don't serve us well, the addictions and dependencies, the obsessions and distractions, in part because they keep us occupied. It's easier to sign onto social media than to sit down in silence and pray. It's easier to buy another gadget, eat another cookie, work another hour than it is to allow ourselves to empty ourselves before the Lord. Being well doesn't require a miracle of the magnitude we see in today's gospel; it just requires a willingness to put aside the things that make us unwell so that Jesus can fill all our empty spaces.

Meditation: Take an inventory of your life today. What eats up most of your time? What makes you unwell, not necessarily physically, but mentally, emotionally, spiritually? What unhealthy thing takes up the space in your heart, mind, and soul that belongs to God? Just for today, try to limit or cut out that thing. How does it feel? Is it freeing or frightening? Give it all to God, whatever you're feeling, and take a first step toward becoming well.

Prayer: God, we so desperately want to be well, but we put obstacles in our own way, barriers that separate us from you. Day by day, help us to let go of our crutches so that we may be made whole in you.

April 3: Wednesday of the Fourth Week of Lent

Peaks and Valleys

Readings: Isa 49:8-15; John 5:17-30

Scripture:
I will cut a road through all my mountains,
   and make my highways level. (Isa 49:11)

Reflection: In upstate New York, the Adirondack Park fans out like a beautiful rolling oasis, drawing hikers, campers, skiers, and all sorts of outdoor enthusiasts in every season. Among that crowd are those known as 46ers, people who have climbed to the summit of each of the Adirondack's forty-six high peaks. Although I've never done more than a few miles of hiking at a time, part of me longs to be in that elite group. The prospect of standing atop the mountains I see only from the comfort of my minivan inspires awe, though the thought is somewhat unrealistic at this point in my life. And so, today's first reading struck a chord as I envisioned not hiking the mountains but driving the highways that hug their sides and look out over sprawling valleys, lakes, and towns.

"I will cut a road through all my mountains, / and make my highways level," we hear in Isaiah. It's no small feat, cutting a road through a mountain, and yet God offers to do this for us so that no matter our age or shape or athletic inclination, we can get where we need to go—closer to him, higher, further up the path that leads us home. There is no elite group when it comes to God. We all have the chance to reach the summit.

Meditation: Is there a high peak looming in your life right now, something that seems too daunting to approach? Are you trying to climb it on your own, or are you willing to let God cut a road through it to ease your way? St. Pope John Paul II said, "The *way Jesus shows you* is *not easy. Rather*, it is *like a path winding up a mountain. Do not lose heart*! The *steeper* the *road*, the *faster* it *rises towards ever wider horizons*." Can you look out at the mountains that dot your life's landscape and see the promise of the summit rather than the depth of the valley? All of life is a holy mountain.

Prayer: Mighty God, only you can lay low the mountains and cut through the obstacles that surround us and keep us stuck in our own worries and fears. Help us to move forward step by step, secure in the knowledge that no path is too difficult if we put our trust in you.

Straight Talk

Readings: Exod 32:7-14; John 5:31-47

Scripture:
The LORD said to Moses,
  "I see how stiff-necked this people is." (Exod 32:9)

Reflection: Things are a little tense in today's readings, to put it mildly. In the first reading from Exodus, the people have given up on God and have created in his stead their own god in the form of a golden calf. Poor Moses has to do some pretty fancy footwork to convince God to step away from the lightning bolts and let the Israelites live. Later, in the Gospel of John, Jesus seems to take a page from his Father's playbook as he lets his listeners know, in no uncertain terms, that he is tired of their disbelief and their refusal to put God first. From our vantage point today, we may think we're above the fray. We haven't built any false gods. Or have we?

Are we "stiff-necked" in our relationship with God, set on our own ways, trying to save ourselves through any number of misguided means? We cling to our material belongings and comforting habits, walking the same worn path in patterns that never take us to the right places. We are not so different from those throwing golden earrings into the fire in hopes of stirring up a solution to life's problems. We are stiff-necked. We like things the way we like them. No thanks,

God, we don't need your help, especially when it takes longer than we expect and doesn't arrive neatly wrapped up exactly as we ordered it, as if prayer were the spiritual equivalent of Amazon Prime. Sometimes we need God to tell it to us straight.

Meditation: What are the false gods you've fashioned? We all have them, whether we admit it or not. They may come in the form of addictions and vices—alcohol, eating, shopping, gambling, scrolling endlessly through social media—or they may be less tangible: control, fear, doubt. False gods don't have to be towering and obvious. In fact, usually they're not. They are small and unassuming, and also insidious because they eat away at our relationship with God while we're not looking. Today, focus on the golden calf in your life and begin to dismantle it bit by bit.

Prayer: God of mercy, we are grateful for your patience with us, for the times you love us through our poor decisions, our distractions, our doubt, and our disregard. We *do* believe your words. Help us to live that truth each day.

One Hundred Kinds of Crazy

Readings: Wis 2:1a, 12-22; John 7:1-2, 10, 25-30

Scripture:
Let us see whether his words be true;
let us find out what will happen to him. (Wis 2:17)

Reflection: "What were they thinking?!?" That's what kept running through my head when I heard today's reading from the book of Wisdom, where people seem to be one hundred kinds of crazy as they go after God's chosen one and put God himself to the test. If we had continued that chapter to its conclusion, we'd get to the heart of the matter: envy, evil.

The devil is certainly in the details of today's first reading and perhaps in the details of our own lives. Do we put God to the test? Has our own wickedness blinded us to the ways in which we sin? "The devil made me do it," we might say jokingly when, in truth, we make the choice to let evil into our lives in great and small ways every day.

Pope Francis regularly reminds Catholics to be alert to the way the devil can slip into our lives without notice. In a daily meditation on February 10, 2017, he said that the devil "fools Eve with his shrewdness: he makes her listen closely . . . she trusts, a dialogue begins and, step after step, he leads her where he wants." He went on to say, "When the devil fools a person, he does so with dialogue; he seeks to dialogue." In other words, the devil sidles up to us like a friend, makes us comfortable, makes temptations seem reasonable—honorable, even—and then, when we are too far in, like Eve standing naked in the garden, we recognize too late the deal we have made.

Meditation: During Lent, when we are making concerted efforts to grow closer to God, the devil seems to pick up the pace. We are suddenly pulled off course by some event or obstacle, thrown into turmoil, darkness, maybe even disbelief. Our Lenten plans may founder and fail, leaving us disappointed in ourselves and, sometimes, in God. And so we may put God to the test, thinking that if God really wants us to become more faithful, it's on him to do the heavy lifting. That's how the devil works, knocking ever so lightly on the door of our soul until we invite him in and leave God out in the cold.

Prayer: Giver of light and love, do not let us be swayed by false promises of ease and comfort when life threatens to derail us. We trust in you today, tomorrow, always.

Seeds of Hatred

Readings: Jer 11:18-20; John 7:40-53

Scripture:
So a division occurred in the crowd because of him.
    (John 7:43)

Reflection: Have you ever done something or said something with the best intentions, perhaps even as a way to
improve a situation, only to find yourself on the receiving
end of animosity or even outright attack? The words you so
carefully planned out ahead of time were misinterpreted or
purposefully twisted to divide people for and against you.
Next thing you know, you're caught in a no-win situation
and wondering how you got there. People hear what they
want to hear, especially when it allows them to avoid a difficult truth.

In today's gospel, we see that human tendency kicked up
a notch as the crowd begins to take sides regarding Jesus.
Where is he from? Who is his family? Is he the Messiah? Is
he a fraud? The guards tell the Pharisees, "Never before has
anyone spoken like this man," recognizing something special
in Jesus. But the Pharisees don't like what they've heard from
Jesus; it's threatening, challenging, condemnable. Little by
little, we see division deepening, widening. We know that
soon it will reach a point of no return, but right now it is

good to stop and take note of how seemingly small seeds of division can blossom into hatred of the hardest and most dangerous kind. We know how it played out in Jesus' story. How will it play out in our own? Do we sow division when we don't like what we hear? Are we prepared to reap what we have sown?

Meditation: The division we see in today's gospel is not so different from the division we see in our world. Fear and misunderstanding mixed with a desire for power too often tear families apart, cause conflict in the workplace, and, on a larger scale, wreak havoc in our world. We can be like the people in today's crowd, thinking with a mob mentality in an effort to maintain control. Are there divisions in your family or in your life that need to be healed? Is there something you could do to begin that process? Can you tear down a wall and build a bridge?

Prayer: God of all, we are one in you, but so often we forget our common bond and focus instead on what divides us. Today we pray for unity and peace. May we begin to heal division one person at a time, starting within our own circle of family and friends.

Sticks and Stones

Readings: Isa 43:16-21; Phil 3:8-14; John 8:1-11

Scripture:
  Woman, where are they?
Has no one condemned you? (John 8:10)

Reflection: The story of the woman caught in adultery is so familiar that it's easy to overlook its significance not only for the woman expecting to be stoned to death, but also for each one of us expecting punishment for the times we have sinned. We may not be waiting for a neighbor to lob a rock at us, but we remain crouched in fear, paralyzed by shame. Sometimes we don't even give God the chance to forgive us. We decide on our own that we are unworthy and deny ourselves the very same mercy that Jesus offers the woman caught in adultery.

  I imagine that woman dragged before Jesus, cowering in fear, head down, arms raised against the painful blows she thought would surely come. She waits—silent, afraid. She knows the punishment for her crime; she does not assume there is a way out. And then, suddenly, mercy, freedom, peace. Jesus' words collapse the angry mob in on itself. "Let the one among you who is without sin be the first to throw a stone at her." And then, "Has no one condemned you? . . . Neither do I condemn you. Go, and from now on do not sin any more." It was that simple and at the same time that incomprehensible. The woman walks away, stunned by the sheer audacity of such a statement. How can this be? And yet the facts bear it out. It is not an empty promise. The mob is gone; the sin is forgiven; the woman is saved, her life changed forever. Do we understand that Jesus holds out the same promise to us today—and every day?

Meditation: Are there things in your life of which you are ashamed? Have you laid them before God and asked for forgiveness, or are you clinging to them, afraid to let God see you for who you are? God already knows. There is nothing to hide and nothing to fear. Jesus shows us this in a fantastic display of mercy in today's gospel. Do you believe you are worthy of the same kind of mercy? We only have to wait and trust Jesus at his word.

Prayer: Jesus, we take shelter in the comfort and peace of your unbounded mercy. We know we are sinners, but you draw us to you all the same, convinced of our worthiness. Thank you for seeing us for who we are and loving us through our sins and failings.

Go Toward the Light

Readings: Dan 13:1-9, 15-17, 19-30, 33-62 or 13:41c-62;
John 8:12-20

Scripture:
I am the light of the world.
Whoever follows me will not walk in darkness,
    but will have the light of life. (John 8:12)

Reflection: If you've ever had to get dressed in a dark room
so as not to wake a sleeping child or spouse, you know how
hard it can be to get it right. You pull the blue pants out of
the closet instead of the black ones. You can't find matching
socks. And forget about trying to put on makeup or style
your hair. If only you could turn on a light, even a nightlight.
Funny how just a flicker in the darkness allows us to move
forward.

When we leave Jesus out of the equation of our daily lives,
it's as though we are perpetually getting dressed in the dark,
walking in the dark. Without Jesus' guiding light we bump
into spiritual walls, make wrong choices, or get so lost that
we just freeze. If we stay in that darkness too long, our eyes
adjust and we fool ourselves into thinking we don't need a
light after all.

For all its benefits, light can be a challenge. It doesn't allow
us to hide. But, if we want to reach our destination, the place

God has set out for us, we need the light of Jesus to lead the way both out in the world and deep inside our souls. It's easy enough, if we're willing. He's right there: in the people we live with, in the strangers we encounter, in both the joyful and frustrating moments, and, most directly, in the Holy Communion we receive at Mass.

Meditation: When was the last time you watched a sunrise? Set an alarm and take a peek, even if it's through a window from the comfort of your own home, even if it's not a picture-perfect sunrise but instead the soft glow that lights up the sky as darkness fades. The morning light doesn't stay contained in a circle on the horizon. It touches everything, casting light on trees and roads and houses. Clouds turn pink; mist becomes visible resting on dew-covered grass; everything changes. Jesus is like that, and you can be like that too. Let the Light touch you and then reflect that light on everyone and everything else on your path today.

Prayer: Jesus, Light of the World, break into our daily life and flood the darkest reaches of our soul. Cast out the darkness that draws us into complacency, and expose the path you have set for us.

Where God Lives

Readings: Num 21:4-9; John 8:21-30

Scripture:
But the one who sent me is true,
    and what I heard from him I tell the world. (John 8:26)

Reflection: I AM. Those simple but powerful words get me every time. It shocks me, in a way, to realize how those two little words shake me to my core whenever I hear them. God lives in those words. And although we first hear them spoken by God himself in Hebrew Scripture, Jesus reminds us of his connection to and oneness with the great I AM in not-so-subtle ways throughout the gospels. "I am the bread of life." "I am the way and the truth and the life." "I am the light of the world." "I am the good shepherd." "I am the vine." "I am the resurrection and the life." In today's gospel Jesus reminds us, too, that everything he says and does comes to him through the Father and that, eventually—perhaps too late— we will recognize that fact and, by extension, Jesus as I AM.

We can sense Jesus' frustration. Sent by the Father, taught by the Father, but so misunderstood by the people he has been sent to save, by all of us. We know Jesus' message. We can quote his most famous teachings verbatim, but we often stop short of recognizing the words as coming not only from Jesus but from God the Father as well. We attribute them to the man Jesus, the faithful teacher, the powerful preacher, but, like the people in today's gospel, we sometimes miss the larger truth.

Meditation: Later in this same chapter of John, Jesus says, "before Abraham came to be, I AM" (John 8:58). There is no getting around what Jesus is saying, and yet, I think we do sometimes try to get around it, maybe not consciously but simply because we're human, and it's hard for humans to grasp the ungraspable. God is I AM; Jesus is I AM. He confounded the people who heard him say it. He confounds us today. What does it mean to you to hear those words, "I AM"? Let them resonate in your mind and heart and spirit throughout the day. Come back to them again and again. Turn them over and excavate them from the confines of Scripture.

Prayer: God the Father, Jesus the Son, Spirit indwelling in all, you are each and all I AM, God before us, God among us, God within us. Let us hear those words and know this truth with every fiber of our being.

Tethered to Half-Truths

Readings: Dan 3:14-20, 91-92, 95; John 8:31-42

Scripture:
   If you remain in my word, you will truly be my disciples,
   and you will know the truth, and the truth will set you
      free. (John 8:31)

Reflection: "Truth" should be clear as a bell, unquestionable, but truth is so often twisted into a mere shadow of itself. We know it all too well these days, when politicians and public figures and social media bubble with a deadly brew of half-truths and outright lies cloaked as truth. We think this is a modern problem, but from the conversation that unfolds in today's gospel, it's clear that truth has always been a complicated topic. Fast forward to what's coming just a week from now, and we will hear the haunting question posed by Pontius Pilate: "What is truth?"

   We might ask ourselves the same question as we reflect on today's gospel: "You shall know the truth, and the truth will set you free." It sounds so simple and straightforward, and yet I don't think I'm alone in saying that I have no clue if I am living the truth, and I certainly don't feel free. I long for that moment; I keep expecting that at some point on this spiritual journey it will become abundantly clear and I will know once and for all my truth, *the* truth. But truth doesn't come with age, like gray hair and wrinkles. If only it did! It comes from the hard work of prayer and discipleship, which is precisely where Jesus started the conversation today. Are we doing our part?

Meditation: Jesus makes clear that knowing the truth and earning the freedom he promises require something of us: faithfulness to the Word. God doesn't simply bestow truth on us like some omnipotent fairy godmother. There is nothing magical about this, which is good news. We have a role in this story because God refuses to force us to accept his word, his truth, his freedom. We have to be willing to invest ourselves in it, to live it, to allow it to run through our veins and out our pores into the world around us. What does truth mean to you? Now take it one step further: What does *the* truth mean to you?

Prayer: God of truth, dispel the false story lines that keep us tethered to a life that is so much less than what you have planned for us. Open our eyes to your truth so that we may taste the freedom that comes from knowing nothing of this world can touch us.

What's in a Word?

Readings: Gen 17:3-9; John 8:51-59

Scripture:
Amen, amen, I say to you,
   whoever keeps my word will never see death. (John 8:51)

Reflection: Continuing on yesterday's theme, Jesus focuses on keeping his word. As a writer, I understand and value the power of words. Written or spoken, carefully crafted or passionately scribbled, the words we humans throw around can move us, scar us, inspire us. Words have weight, even without the power of God behind them. And then we get to the Word, which we recognize, with just the touch of a shift key raising that first letter, to be Logos, God incarnate in the person of Jesus, who has existed for all time since before all time along with the Father and Spirit.

   The Word gives us his word and asks us to keep it. How beautiful. Such a gift. How could we possibly say no? But we do, again and again. We say no to the notion of loving others as we love ourselves when it becomes too difficult, no to caring for the poor and hungry when it makes us uncomfortable, no to peace when we want to win an argument or a war, no to turning the other cheek when the world urges us to strike back, no to trusting in God's plan when it seems to be going in a direction we don't like. Remaining in Jesus' word sounds very good on paper, but real life is a different story. Today Jesus gets right to the point: keep his word; never die. Shouldn't that promise be enough to change our hearts and minds and actions in one fell swoop? What will it take to get it to sink in?

Meditation: In *The Cloud of Unknowing*, one of the great spiritual classics on prayer, the anonymous author says, "This kingdom of heaven is your heritage, and God asks you to claim it. . . . God waits for your cooperation." We are told throughout Scripture that eternal life, salvation, the kingdom of heaven are ours for the taking if we but follow the way Jesus sets out for us. All it takes is our cooperation. Today, sit down in prayer and silently reflect on this great mystery. Can you do one thing today to keep Jesus' word, to cooperate with the divine plan?

Prayer: Jesus, we stand before you today willing but unsure. We are so easily pulled off course by the stresses of this life. We know your word is truth and life. Help us to hold fast to your promises.

We Have a Champion

Readings: Jer 20:10-13; John 10:31-42

Scripture:
I hear the whisperings of many . . .
But the LORD is with me, like a mighty champion . . . "
   (Jer 20:10-11)

Reflection: Whispers can be withering to the spirit, whether you're a kid on a playground or a grown-up in an office. The sight of someone speaking in hushed tones behind the shield of a raised hand can undo even the most put-together person, even a prophet. We see in today's first reading that Jeremiah is no stranger to the all-too-human insecurities that surface when the whispering begins and, in his case, builds to a near-silent scream of insults and threats. The fear is palpable as he recounts their words. And then, within a few lines, Jeremiah's resolve returns and the doubts vanish. He has God on his side. He has no reason to fear. He has a champion.

   Each one of us has the same champion, although we tend to forget that. We allow ourselves to stay in that place of fear, letting the whispers echo and strengthen, feeding them with our own insecurities until they grow into something we don't know how to face. Jeremiah is a great one to remind us that difficult times do not have to end badly. In fact, difficult times are par for the course, and God, our champion, waits to take up our cause if we'll let him. We can't stop the whispers. All we can control is our reaction to them. If we're willing to look to God and trust what God has in store for us, the rest will fall into place. We will find a peace that cannot be shaken by murmurs or threats.

Meditation: Pay attention today, this week, to the ways you feel injured by or at risk from people around you: harsh words, a whisper, maybe just a look. It's okay to feel that way. After all, even Jeremiah the prophet wasn't immune to the pain such things can cause. But don't stay in that place. Push through to the other side, where God is waiting to be your champion. You do not have to react to the whispers. You do not have to invest any energy in someone else's story. Stick with what you can control: your own actions grounded in your relationship with God.

Prayer: All-powerful God, I know that you are always at my side, no matter how difficult my struggles, no matter how alone I may feel. I trust in you, and I thank you for your unwavering love for me.

April 13: Saturday of the Fifth Week of Lent

A Shadow of a Doubt

Readings: Ezek 37:21-28; John 11:45-56

Scripture:
If we leave him alone, all will believe in him . . . (John 11:48)

Reflection: With the raising of Lazarus still fresh in their minds, the leaders of the Jewish community around Jesus are getting nervous. The signs are too great, the risks too high. People are starting to believe. How could they not? This man cures the blind and lame; this man raises people from the dead. They cannot allow this to threaten the status quo and their comfort and power along with it. And so doubts are sown, outright lies told, dire predictions made. True to human form, the people who believed because their own eyes had seen begin to waver. Maybe it wasn't real. Maybe he is dangerous. Maybe we're crazy for jumping on this bandwagon.

The same sort of thing goes on in our world today. We know what we believe and why we believe it, but there are many who would cast us as fools, gullible bumpkins not smart enough to see the light. Believing in something we can't see and touch, trusting that our life will continue long after our physical body wears out, basing our entire life on the words and actions of a man who lived two thousand years ago and claimed to be one with God—maybe we, too, are crazy for jumping on this bandwagon. The thought crosses our mind, fleetingly, when the drumbeat of the world gets so loud it drowns out the still small voice. If that begins to happen, come back to Scripture, Eucharist, prayer, and community, and remember what drew you to this faith in the first place and what keeps you firmly rooted.

Meditation: It's hard to admit the doubts we may have to ourselves, much less to anyone else. Won't they be scandalized? Won't they think less of me? Truth is, doubts come with the territory and, in fact, can propel us forward on our spiritual journey, if we are willing to pay attention and face them rather than hide in fear. Pope Francis has said, "We do not need to be afraid of questions and doubts because they are the beginning of a path of knowledge and going deeper."

Prayer: This journey toward heaven is fraught with beautiful summits and dangerous blind spots, stretches of ease and backbreaking climbs. Through it all, we return to you, Father, sure that you are beside us, even when those around us try to convince us otherwise. We believe!

Beyond Our Grasp

Readings: Luke 19:28-40; Isa 50:4-7; Phil 2:6-11; Luke 22:14–23:56 or 23:1-49

Scripture:
Christ Jesus, though he was in the form of God,
  did not regard equality with God
  something to be grasped. (Phil 2:6)

Reflection: As we enter Holy Week, we do so knowing full well what's ahead and how quickly we humans can take goodness and light and snuff it out, all for our own benefit. Jesus rides into Jerusalem on a wave of hosannas, palm fronds bowing in adulation, but in a matter of days, the praise and glory will be trampled under the weight of self-preservation fueled by fear. A deadly combination. Jesus, God among us, will quietly, willingly suffer what we demand through our broken humanity and twisted sense of self.

Which brings us to today's second reading, a powerful and poetic verse outlining a harsh reality we read but cannot fully assimilate. Jesus "did not regard equality with God / something to be grasped." The Son of God did not attempt to put himself on equal footing with God the Father. If only we humans could do the same. Since the dawn of creation, humans have attempted to make ourselves into gods, to put ourselves on equal footing with the One who created us and the One who died for us. And God, in his infinite mercy, not only allows it but continues to embrace us in spite of it, which is how we end up at Palm Sunday and all that is to come this week, looking up at a cross on which we have hung the Savior of the world because he did not live up to our expectations. Jesus could not grasp equality with God, but, somehow, we find a way. It's remarkable, really, that we can be so bold in the face of the One who is and was and is to come.

Meditation: When was the last time you approached God with good old-fashioned awe and wonder, not because you had a specific prayer answered but just because God is God. Today, spend some time with this Scripture verse and ponder what it would mean to empty yourself out before God, before Jesus, with heartfelt humility and gratitude. What would that look like? Can you stop trying to take the controls and let God be God?

Prayer: Father, forgive us for our indiscretions, our human weaknesses, the same weaknesses that led the throng to yell, "Crucify him." We bow our heads at the mention of Jesus' name, knowing we are not worthy and yet are loved beyond measure. Help us never to forget that beautiful truth.

April 15: Monday of Holy Week

God's Extravagant Love

Readings: Isa 42:1-7; John 12:1-11

Scripture:
Mary took a liter of costly perfumed oil
    made from genuine aromatic nard
    and anointed the feet of Jesus and dried them with her hair;
    the house was filled with the fragrance of the oil. (John 12:3)

Reflection: What an outrageous and magnificent display of love we see in today's gospel. Although the practical types, Judas among them, tsk-tsked at the apparent waste of valuable oil, Mary knew better. There was nothing too good for the Messiah, nothing that should be spared or withheld—not because he demanded extravagance but because his very presence demanded an extraordinary response, one that could be fulfilled only by an action above and beyond our wildest expectations. Imagine for a moment that scene in today's gospel. Imagine a woman walking into a room and not only pouring oil over the feet of the guest of honor but then drying his feet with her hair. Her hair. So much humility, honor, devotion, love in that gesture. Where would she have found the courage to make such a bold statement, to put her reputation on the line in order to do what needed to be done? And we hear that the fragrance filled the house. There was no containing this action, this moment; it spread into every corner until everything within striking distance was infused with the scent.

And Jesus does not stop her. He does not put up his hand and say, "No, no." Instead he rebukes Judas, saying, "You always have the poor with you, but you do not always have me." Mary must have felt relieved at those words, and perhaps confused, although her action shows that she understood far more than Judas did. Hers was a quiet, constant devotion that eventually spilled over, carried along by perfumed oil.

Meditation: Has there ever been a time when your faith prompted you to do something outrageous or beyond practicality? Perhaps you left a job to follow a calling, donated more than was reasonable to a worthy cause, put aside every fear and trusted completely during a difficult time, cried uncontrollable tears at the recognition of God's presence in your life. And perhaps someone questioned it. Own that action today, not with pride but with pure joy for the gift that it was. Whenever we do something outrageous in service to God, we can be sure the Spirit is at work!

Prayer: Our God is an awesome God, a God of extravagance and abundance and more than enough. Thank you, God, for sending us the Spirit who, like perfumed oil, fills the gaps and voids in our souls with the perfume of your unending love.

Pivotal Moments

Readings: Isa 49:1-6; John 13:21-33, 36-38

Scripture:
After Judas took the morsel, Satan entered him.
So Jesus said to him, "What you are going to do, do
   quickly." (John 13:27)

Reflection: Darkness surrounds us as we imagine the pain
Jesus felt, knowing his betrayer was breaking bread with
him. Judas hears Jesus announce his betrayal and still doesn't
recognize the moment for what it is: one last opportunity to
choose good over evil, salvation over suffering. "After Judas
took the morsel, Satan entered him." We have the sense that
right up until that very second, there was another way, but
Judas does not stop to reconsider. Was he so convinced of
what he was doing that he could not even see the betrayal
embedded in it? Was he so evil he didn't care? We will never
know, but what we do know is that at some point, Judas'
commitment to what he is about to do becomes flush with
the power of evil personified. Satan entered him. The words
send a shudder down our spine. How easily Satan enters
into our midst, our minds, our motivations when we let
down our guard.

Maybe Satan doesn't enter into us with quite the force and
power as he did Judas that night, but does Satan make small

and steady inroads without us even realizing it, every time we knowingly choose self over other, wrong over right, convenience over conscience? "This is evil, it is not a diffuse concept, it's a person," Pope Francis has said of Satan. "With Satan you can't argue."

Meditation: For many of us in the modern world, Satan seems to be part of a bygone era, a shocking symbol of evil meant to scare us away from bad behavior. But holy men and women throughout history have told us otherwise. Jesus tells us otherwise. We have seen Jesus himself tempted by the devil. So powerful is Satan that even the Son of God can be tempted. What makes us think we are beyond Satan's grasp? We are not. Judas recognized too late what he had done and, rather than seek God's mercy, allowed Satan to give him one last push into the abyss of darkness. Let his example remind us to always be on guard against the evil that enters so easily and then refuses to leave.

Prayer: Jesus, Light of the World, shine your love into my life and cast out the shadows of darkness that lurk there. Give me the strength to withstand the evil that laps at the shore of my soul.

Shamed

Readings: Isa 50:4-9a; Matt 26:14-25

Scripture:
The Lord GOD is my help,
   therefore I am not disgraced;
I have set my face like flint,
   knowing that I shall not be put to shame. (Isa 50:7)

Reflection: In the world's eyes, at least at the time, Jesus *was* put to shame. People couldn't understand how the man who could save others could not save himself. It looked like the ultimate defeat: the Son of God, the Christ, the Messiah, hanging from a cross between two thieves. Even among the disciples in the crowd—the few who were brave enough to hang around—there had to be a sense of disbelief. How could it end this way? Why wouldn't God rescue him, show the world that this was, in fact, his beloved Son? But Jesus, as prophesied in Isaiah, does not fight back, does not attempt to save himself, does not even ask his Father to save him. Yes, he cries out in anguish, asking the Father why he has abandoned him, but we know that even then he trusted that this would end not in shame and disgrace but in victory and everlasting life. He allowed himself to be humiliated and tortured and shamed for our sake, for the good of humanity.

Few of us are willing to be shamed for any reason, especially when we've done nothing to bring the shame upon ourselves. We may be willing to make ourselves a little uncomfortable to do something generous for someone else, but shame and disgrace? That's another story. When we do good things, we expect praise, not derision, and yet sometimes that is what we are called to accept, knowing that the right thing will be seen by God even if it is not seen by our neighbor.

Meditation: What do shame and disgrace bring up for you? A specific event or just a general sense of unease? Have you ever been shamed by someone for something you did with the best of intentions? Imagine what it must have felt like for Jesus, hanging from a cross, mocked and shamed, knowing he had the power to undo it all in an instant but willing to bear it in order to fulfill God's plan. How much are we willing to suffer to fulfill God's plan in our own lives?

Prayer: Lord of all faithfulness, we are afraid of suffering, but we trust that, even when we feel alone and abandoned by the world, you are beside us. You will not let us be put to shame. Help us to remember that in our darkest hours.

We Are One Body

Readings: Exod 12:1-8, 11-14; 1 Cor 11:23-26; John 13:1-15

Scripture:
This is my body that is for you.
Do this in remembrance of me. (1 Cor 11:24)

Reflection: Eucharist—heavenly food given to us at an earthly banquet—is at the heart of what we commemorate today and at the heart of our Christian lives every day. Still, it can be so difficult to grasp in a concrete way. I always imagine that if any of us could truly grasp what is happening on the altar, what is placed in our hand or on our tongue, we would lie prostrate before the altar in awe and gratitude. But God gives us this gift knowing full well we cannot possibly understand the magnitude of what we are receiving.

St. Augustine, in his sermon on Eucharist said, "Be what you can see, and receive what you are." That's probably a surprising piece of spiritual advice for many of us: to receive what we are. It implies something powerful, something we have not, perhaps, taken the time to assimilate into our hearts and minds and souls. Do we truly see ourselves as the Body of Christ?

In a homily on the Feast of Corpus Christi in 2010, Pope Benedict XVI put St. Augustine's advice into practical terms: "By nourishing ourselves with him in the Eucharist and by receiving the Holy Spirit in our hearts, we truly form the Body of Christ that we have received, we are truly in communion with him and with each other and genuinely become his instruments, bearing witness to him before the world."

Today, as we commemorate the Last Supper and the first Eucharist, try to see things from Augustine's perspective.

Meditation: The next time you receive Holy Communion, make a little extra effort to put yourself in the right frame of mind. Don't worry about how long the line is or that the choir might be singing that favorite hymn too slowly. Don't look at your watch or talk to your spouse. Just close your eyes and focus on what is about to happen. What do you feel as you approach the altar? What does this sacrament mean to you? The Eucharist unites us not only with Christ but also with one another, the Body of Christ. Receive what you are.

Prayer: Lord, Jesus, I believe you are truly present in the Eucharist. May this unearned gift infuse my life with the desire to become more fully what you have created me to be, to become your hands and feet at work in the world.

Living in Denial

Readings: Isa 52:13–53:12; Heb 4:14-16; 5:7-9; John 18:1–19:42

Scripture:
Now Simon Peter was standing there keeping warm.
And they said to him,
   "You are not one of his disciples, are you?"
He denied it and said,
   "I am not." (John 18:25)

Reflection: Today is a day of darkness, death, and denial.
This is where we end up when we allow fear to rule our
hearts. Darkness moves like a slow, rolling fog through the
valleys of our lives and settles there, clouding our vision,
much as it did that day for the Pharisees and Sanhedrin, for
Pontius Pilate and Simon Peter, for every person in the crowd
who screamed, "Crucify him!" It may seem that power,
rather than fear, was at work. After all, only power gone mad
can have a man scourged, crowned with thorns, and hung
on a cross. But the truth is that fear, not power, does those
things. Real power lifts where fear oppresses. Real power
resurrects where fear destroys. Peter found that out the hard
way, and it's in him that we find hope for ourselves as we
struggle toward Calvary today.

   We see him warming his hands and denying the Messiah,
and it seems as though all hope is lost. Even Peter. Although

we don't have the details of what happened after the cock crowed and Peter realized what he had done, we can make an educated guess. No doubt, it wasn't pretty. Locked away in desperation and self-disgust, the story could have ended there for Peter. But it does not. While darkness may rule the day, we know it does not have the last word. Not for Peter, and not for us, if we allow God's power to do its work in our lives.

Meditation: The sorrow of Good Friday is palpable. We can feel it in our bones. Even the prayers of the Church and the Liturgy of Good Friday ache with the pain of what has occurred on Calvary, this unspeakable act that results in unending life for all of us. God writes straight with crooked lines. The cross becomes a symbol of life. Death becomes the doorway to eternity. Is there darkness anywhere in your life today? Can you look to the cross and see the sliver of light trying to break in? Hold tight to the cross, and the darkness will not win.

Prayer: Lamb of God, broken and battered on our behalf, forgive us for the times we have doubted and denied. We trust in your mercy. We lift high the cross. We thank you for facing down the fear and transforming it into new life for us.

Infinitely Beautiful

Readings: Gen 1:1–2:2 or 1:1, 26-31a; Gen 22:1-18 or 22:1-2, 9a, 10-13, 15-18; Exod 14:15–15:1; Isa 54:5-14; Isa 55:1-11; Bar 3:9-15, 32–4:4; Ezek 36:16-17a, 18-28; Rom 6:3-11; Luke 24:1-12

Scripture:
Why do you seek the living one among the dead?
He is not here, but he has been raised. (Luke 24:5-6)

Reflection: A monk at the Abbey of the Genesee in western New York asked me, during a spiritual direction session, to consider the meaning of the infinite, the eternal, a God beyond all time. "When you deal with God, you enter another world," said Fr. John Eudes Bamberger, perhaps best known for being taught by the most famous Trappist, Thomas Merton, and later for serving as spiritual director to writer and theologian Henri Nouwen. Throughout our hour-long session, he kept coming back to death and the fact that it could show up unbidden at any moment.

That retreat experience came flooding back as I read today's gospel. The women at the tomb, confused by the absence of a body. The disciples in hiding, confused by the story the women told: "their story seemed like nonsense and they did not believe them." (Luke 24:11) There is much confusion today. None of it makes sense. How can this be? Because we are dealing with God, and when we deal with God, we have to check our human sensibilities at the door. On this day of waiting, we ponder the infinite, which just yesterday seemed impossible. God makes a way where there was none before. This much we know. We live every day by acts of faith, the old monk told me as I sat before him, full of confusion and doubt, a modern version of the disbelieving disciples, "We have to trust," he said. Today more than ever.

Meditation: Holy Saturday offers a quiet beauty as we move through the emptiness of the liturgical day toward the new fire of the Easter Vigil and the emptiness of the tomb. It is a day to trust even when logic tells us otherwise. Can you trust the men in the garden asking us why we are looking for the living one among the dead? Can you trust the women who say Jesus is not there; he has been raised? Can you trust that what we await on Holy Saturday is what we await when we eventually leave this world? Today, ponder the infinite. If you dare, ponder your own death, and then go out and live by acts of faith.

Prayer: Eternal God, we believe in your promise of salvation. Flood our hearts with trust and open our eyes to the dazzling reality of the infinite sustaining us even now.

April 21: Easter Sunday: The Resurrection of the Lord

Alleluia! Alleluia!

Readings: Acts 10:34a, 37-43; Col 3:1-4 or 1 Cor 5:6b-8; John 20:1-9 or Luke 24:1-12 or, at an afternoon or evening Mass, Luke 24:13-35

Scripture:
Then the other disciple also went in,
  the one who had arrived at the tomb first,
  and he saw and believed. (John 20:8)

Reflection: We awake today to a shift so seismic, it's a wonder the earth didn't a bobble a bit on its axis. Jesus Christ is risen today. Alleluia! Alleluia! It's as though someone has thrown open the world's windows. The earthy scent of new life mixed with the heady scent of Easter lilies rushes through and makes us swoon. It seems too good to be true, and yet we know this is what Jesus has earned for us. Brokenness has been transformed into beauty, death into life, sorrow into joy. Although we've known all along how Calvary would end, it still takes us by surprise come Easter morning. Our God became human, died for us, and rose to new life so that we might never die. That's a truth that never gets old. We see and we believe!

But believing is not the end of this. As we hear in the Acts of the Apostles, Jesus wants us to preach, to testify to this truth. That is our calling, our mission, not just on Easter but every day of our lives. Not just in church but at the dinner table, at the water cooler, on social media, on the soccer field, in the grocery line, and everywhere else we go. We don't have to give a prepared speech or even speak at all. We simply have to let our everyday actions speak to the truth we know in our hearts: Jesus Christ is our Lord and Savior. He came to save every one of us simply because he loves us just as we are, for all time until the end of time. Amen, amen. Alleluia, amen!

Meditation: We stand at the start of the Easter season. How will you take the joy that fills your heart today out into the world tomorrow and every day after? Can you think of some daily practices that will help you live this Easter joy more fully? Perhaps the Lenten practice you began on Ash Wednesday has turned into a much-loved habit that can be woven into "regular" life. Or maybe there is a new spiritual practice that can become the focus of the next fifty days as we journey toward Pentecost. Live your joy!

Prayer: Risen Lord, we come to you today filled with awe and gratitude, humility and joy. We thank you for this gift of new life and this promise of hope.

References

March 30: Saturday of the Third Week of Lent
Thomas Merton, *No Man Is an Island* (Boston: Shambhala, 2005), 119.

April 3: Wednesday of the Fourth Week of Lent
John Paul II, Message of the Holy Father Pope John Paul II for the XI World Youth Day, November 26, 1995, http:// w2.vatican.va/content/john-paul-ii/en/messages/youth /documents/hf_jp-ii_mes_26111995_xi-world-youth-day .html.

April 5: Friday of the Fourth Week of Lent
Pope Francis, Morning Meditation in the Chapel of the *Domus Sanctae Marthae*: How to Respond to Temptation, February 10, 2017, https://w2.vatican.va/content/francesco/en/cotidie /2017/documents/papa-francesco-cotidie_20170210_how -to-respond-to-temptation.html.

April 11: Thursday of the Fifth Week of Lent
Anonymous, *The Cloud of Unknowing* (Brewster, MA: Paraclete Press, 2016), chap. 2, p. 4.

April 13: Saturday of the Fifth Week of Lent
Cindy Wooden, "Pope Francis Says Doubt Is Key to Life of Faith," *Crux*, November 23, 2016, https://cruxnow.com

/vatican/2016/11/23/pope-francis-says-doubt-key-life
-faith/.

April 16: Tuesday of Holy Week
Samuel Osborne, "Pope Francis Says Satan Is a Very Smart
Person You Should Not Argue With," *Independent*, December
14, 2017, http://www.independent.co.uk/news/world
/europe/pope-francis-satan-devil-person-argue-smart-tv
2000-catholic-broadcasting-network-a8110621.html.

April 18: Holy Thursday (Maundy Thursday)
Augustine of Hippo, *Sermon 272*, in *Sermons*, pt. 3, vol. 7, ed.
John E. Rotelle, trans. Edmund Hill, OP, 300–301 (Hyde Park:
New City Press, 1993), http://www.stanselminstitute.org
/files/Augustine,%20Sermon%20272.pdf.

Pope Benedict, Holy Mass on the Occasion of the Publication
of the *Instrumentum Laboris* of the Special Assembly for the
Middle East of the Synod of Bishops, Apostolic Journey to
Cyprus, June 6, 2010, https://w2.vatican.va/content
/benedict-xvi/en/homilies/2010/documents/hf_ben-xvi
_hom_20100606_instr-laboris.pdf.